Every Body Has Something to Say

Written by

Monica Ashour, MTS, MHum

Illustrated by

Marilee Harrald-Pilz

Pauline

BOOKS & MEDIA

Boston

Library of Congress Cataloging-in-Publication Data

Ashour, Monica.
  Every body has something to say / written by Monica Ashour, MTS, M Hum ;
illustrated by Marilee Harrald-Pilz.
      pages cm
  Summary: "This book makes children aware of how their bodies speak to
them and to others"-- Provided by publisher.
  ISBN 978-0-8198-2385-4 (soft cover) -- ISBN 0-8198-2385-6 (soft cover)
  1. Human body--Religious aspects--Catholic Church. 2. Body language.
I. Harrald-Pilz, Marilee. II. Title.
  BX1795.B63A84 2015
  233'.5--dc23
                          2014046155

Cover and interior design by Mary Joseph Peterson, FSP

Text copyright © 2015, Monica Ashour

Illustrations copyright © 2015, Daughters of St. Paul

"P" and PAULINE are registered trademarks of the Daughters of St. Paul.

Published by Pauline Books & Media, 50 Saint Pauls Avenue, Boston, MA
02130–3491

Printed in U.S.A.

EBSS VSAUSAPEOILL2-1710034 2385-6

www.pauline.org

1 2 3 4 5 6 7 8 9   19 18 17 16 15

Note to Parents, Guardians, and Teachers

Most of us are familiar with the term "body language." Simply put, we communicate with our bodies. Saint John Paul II, however, took the concept to a whole new level and direction. *This book* makes accessible what Saint John Paul II called the "language of the body." The four foundational principles of the Theology of the Body that are presented in these pages will unlock the beauty, power, and purpose of the body in God's plan for each of us—and for the children entrusted to our care.

- **We must "listen" to what the body has to say.** By submitting to our needs for rest, nourishment, and safety, we learn to become attentive and begin to discern between needs and wants.

- **We have the ability to choose whether, when, and how to respond to the body.** What Saint John Paul II calls "self-mastery" enables us to develop Christian virtue. It moves us toward the freedom necessary for true self-giving love. Practicing self-mastery before the challenges of adolescence prepares kids to live those meanings honestly throughout their lives.

- **The body "speaks" objective truth.** Laughter means "I think something is funny"; it *can't* mean "I am extremely sad." Bodily actions have deep meaning attached to them.

- **Our inner life is revealed by our outer action.** Contrary to our society's message, our bodies are not tools or shells. As Saint John Paul II puts it, the body is a "sacrament" of each person.

Drawing young children's attention to the body's meaning affirms the innate goodness of the body and its "message." Further, as a child's body and soul become more fully integrated, he or she becomes more capable of communicating love to others and to the God who created each of us in his image.

For more information and teaching ideas for this and other Theology of the Body principles, please visit www.pauline.org/tob4children.

Bodies talk and bodies listen.

Every body has something to say!

My body talks! It tells me all kinds of things.

Grumble, grumble.

My growling tummy tells me I'm hungry.

Yaaaawwwn.

My stretching mouth
tells me I'm tired.

Brrrrrrr.

My shivering
arms tell me
I'm cold.

Aaaachoooo!

My runny nose
tells me I'm
getting sick.

Thump, thump, thump!

My pounding heart
tells me I'm scared
of the dark.

Ouuuuuch!

My burning
knee tells me
I'm hurt.

Bodies talk and bodies listen.

Every body has something to say!

I listen to my body, but I think about what I hear.

Sometimes I do what my body tells me right away. Other times I decide it is better to wait.

I'm hungry, but I can choose to
eat later because dinnertime is soon,
and I don't want to spoil my appetite.

I'm tired, and I can choose to go to bed early and get the rest I need.

I'm cold, but I can choose to put on a warm coat and play a little longer.

I'm getting sick, and I can choose to rest and ask if my parents think I need to go to the doctor.

9

I'm scared, but I can choose to be brave,
think of good things, and say a prayer.

I'm hurt, and I can choose
to ask someone to help me.

Bodies talk and bodies listen.

Every body has something to say!

My body doesn't talk to just me. And your body doesn't talk to just you. . . .

Bodies can listen to each other.

When tears well up in my friend's eyes and roll down his cheeks, his body is telling me he's sad.

When the girl who lives next door giggles,
and giggles, and giggles some more, her body
is telling me she thinks something's funny.

When my baby cousin's eyelids are heavy and won't stay open, his body is telling me he's tired.

When my teammate bounces her leg, or rubs her forehead, or paces back and forth, or bites her nails, her body is telling me she's worried.

When I stamp my feet very loudly
or put my hands on my hips, my body
is saying I'm angry or upset.

When I look down at the floor as
I talk to my friend, my body is saying
that I'm sorry.

When I smile at my teacher, my body is saying that I like her.

When I hug my grandpa tightly with both arms and hold on for a very long time, my body is telling him that I love him.

Bodies talk and bodies listen.

Every body has something to say!

Bodies don't use words; they have their own language.

They speak with hands and feet, with arms and legs and eyes.

Our bodies tell us what we need to know and show our inside selves to others.

Bodies talk and bodies listen.

Every body has something to say!

Monica Ashour

National speaker, former teacher, and executive director of the Theology of the Body Evangelization Team (TOBET), Monica Ashour makes the depth and breadth of Saint John Paul II's revolutionary Theology of the Body (TOB) accessible. Building on her **TOB for Tots** series, Monica, who holds two master's degrees from the University of Dallas in the humanities and theological studies, goes one step deeper in **TOB for Kids**. These books make the mystery of the human person visible in the context of Catholic faith. Young and old alike will learn to see the BODY rightly: as a gift from God and a call to love. For more resources from TOBET, go to www.tobet.org.

Marilee Harrald-Pilz

Marilee Harrald-Pilz has been working as a freelance illustrator since 1979. After graduating from the University of Illinois with a BA in art education, she attended the Chicago Academy of Art, the American Academy of Art, and the School of the Art Institute of Chicago. A proud member of the Picture Book Artists Association, Marilee has primarily focused on the illustration of books, educational materials, magazines, and greetings cards for children. As a senior illustrator at Diamond Toy Company, she illustrated licensed characters, packaging, and display cards. Marilee has also worked as a designer of educational products at Cook Communications Ministries and Scripture Press Publications.

Marilee's work can be seen at:
www.MarileeHarrald-Pilz.com,
and www.storybookartsinc.com

Positively Human

kids *Pauline*

Our Positively Human Line offers an affirmative view of the human person while integrating faith concepts for kids.

Everybody Has a Body
God Made Boys and Girls
Written by Monica Ashour
Illustrated by Karol Kaminski

God Made Wonderful Me!
Written by Genny Monchamp
Illustrated by Karol Kaminski

Every Body Is Smart
God Helps Me Listen and Choose
Written by Monica Ashour
Illustrated by Karol Kaminski

God Has a Plan for Boys and for Girls
Written by Monica Ashour
Illustrated by Marilee Harrald-Pilz

Every Body Has Something to Say

Every Body Is a Gift
God Made Us to Love
Written by Monica Ashour
Illustrated by Karol Kaminski

Everybody Has Something to Give
Written by Monica Ashour
Illustrated by Marilee Harrald-Pilz

Coming Soon!
Mommy, Am I Strong?
Daddy, Am I Beautiful?

To find these and other delightful books for children, visit one of our **Pauline Books & Media** centers listed on the next page or stop by: www.pauline.org. We'd love to hear from you!

Pauline
BOOKS & MEDIA

The Daughters of St. Paul operate book and media centers at the following addresses. Visit, call, or write the one nearest you today, or find us at www.pauline.org.

CALIFORNIA
3908 Sepulveda Blvd, Culver City, CA 90230 — 310-397-8676
935 Brewster Avenue, Redwood City, CA 94063 — 650-369-4230
5945 Balboa Avenue, San Diego, CA 92111 — 858-565-9181

FLORIDA
145 SW 107th Avenue, Miami, FL 33174 — 305-559-6715

HAWAII
1143 Bishop Street, Honolulu, HI 96813 — 808-521-2731

ILLINOIS
172 North Michigan Avenue, Chicago, IL 60601 — 312-346-4228

LOUISIANA
4403 Veterans Memorial Blvd, Metairie, LA 70006 — 504-887-7631

MASSACHUSETTS
885 Providence Hwy, Dedham, MA 02026 — 781-326-5385

MISSOURI
9804 Watson Road, St. Louis, MO 63126 — 314-965-3512

NEW YORK
64 West 38th Street, New York, NY 10018 — 212-754-1110

SOUTH CAROLINA
243 King Street, Charleston, SC 29401 — 843-577-0175

TEXAS
Currently no book center; for parish exhibits or outreach evangelization, contact: 210-569-0500 or SanAntonio@paulinemedia.com

VIRGINIA
1025 King Street, Alexandria, VA 22314 — 703-549-3806

CANADA
3022 Dufferin Street, Toronto, ON M6B 3T5 — 416-781-9131

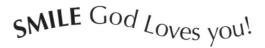

SMILE God Loves you!